Better H

Repairing
Furniture

GREG CHEETHAM

MINI · WORKBOOK · SERIES

MURDOCH BOOKS®
Sydney • London • Vancouver • New York

CONTENTS

*A restored writing box (top), a chair with missing parts
(far left), and the chair with the parts replaced (left)*

SPECIES OF TIMBER

Blackwood

Blackbutt

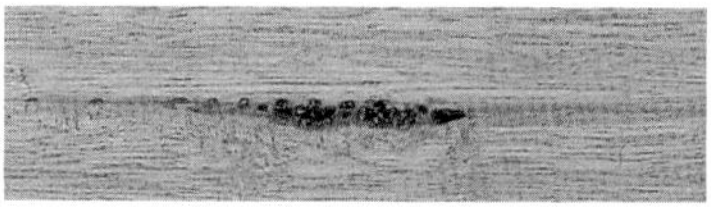

Flooded gum

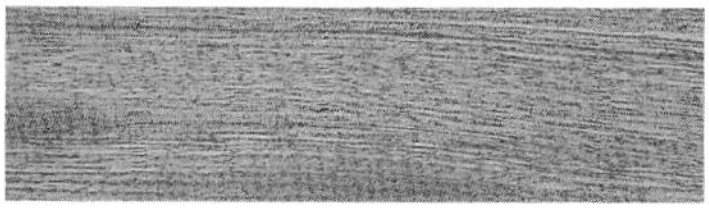

Sapele

American white oak

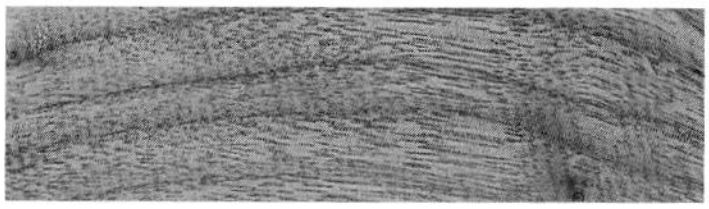

American walnut

American cherry

Kwila

Steamed European beech

Teak

Brazilian mahogany

Anagre

Jeltong

Queensland maple

Before you begin

Identifying the species of timber used in a piece of furniture is the first step in the repair process. A knowledge of construction techniques will also give you a head start when it comes to repairs.

TIMBER

There are two main types of timber: hardwoods and softwoods. The hardwoods have large pores—cells used for storing moisture and food. These are generally visible on the surface once the timber has been dressed (had its surfaces planed smooth). Most hardwoods are from deciduous trees, which lose their leaves in autumn.

Softwoods have a more even cell structure than hardwoods and are usually evergreen, cone-bearing trees with needle-like leaves.

Five main characteristics can be used to identify a species of timber. These characteristics are:
• colour
• grain pattern
• texture
• figure
• smell

COLOUR

Many species of timber are a similar colour, so this characteristic cannot be used on its own to distinguish one type of timber from another. However, it can be used in conjunction with other characteristics to determine the species of a timber. The colour of a species of timber can vary slightly, depending on such factors as soil condition and from which layer of the tree it was cut.

Heartwood (timber taken from the core of a tree) will generally be darker than sapwood (timber taken from the outer layers).

GRAIN PATTERN

The grain pattern of a piece of timber is formed by growth rings—light and dark rings on the end of the timber. These indicate the growth and dormant seasons in the timber's life cycle.

In the growing season, rapid expansion results in a tree's cells being loosely packed and its growth rings are usually light in colour. Darker rings indicate a season with less rapid expansion and a tighter cell structure. Sections of timber with dark growth rings are harder than those with light rings.

The grain pattern of certain timbers can be very pronounced. Radiata pine, for instance, has a well-defined grain pattern which takes the form of stripes of light and dark rings on the surface of the timber. Other varieties of pine, for example kauri pine, have grain patterns that are quite uniform.

TEXTURE

This is the feel of the dressed surface, for example, whether it is rough or smooth. The texture of a piece of dressed timber can be determined by moving the tips of the fingers lightly over it.

The porosity or density of the grain structure creates a timber's texture. A timber such as American white oak has a rougher texture than, for example, kauri pine.

The texture of a piece of timber is an important consideration when it comes to deciding what finishing technique to use. Rough-textured timber needs more polish to achieve a flat finish than fine-textured timber.

Certain finishing techniques, such as using a wood-grain filler to help fill the pores before applying polish, will make finishing rough-textured timber quicker.

FIGURE

The pattern of the grain of a piece of timber is known as the figure. The figure of timber grain may result from the growing conditions of the timber.

One example of this is bird's-eye maple, which is a type of American rock maple. This is characterised by tight clusters of swirling grain. These clusters form what appear to be knots on the surface of a board, but they may only penetrate a few millimetres.

Another example is fiddleback. This is the name given when the surface grain has a wavy appearance and an uneven texture. Fiddleback may only occur in some parts of a log, the remaining parts of the log may have straight grain.

The figure of timber grain can also be caused by the conversion of the timber to boards. Boards with growth rings tangential to the face, for example, will have highly figured face patterns, while boards with growth rings at 90 degrees to the face will not be figured.

SMELL

The oils contained in some timbers cause them to exude strong, distinctive smells which can be used to determine their species.

Camphor laurel, for example, has a sharp odour that many people will be familiar with, as does oregon and Australian red cedar. Some timbers have such noxious scents they can make people with sensitive noses ill. Blackbean is one such Australian timber.

The best way to test the scent of a timber is to smell a freshly cut piece or to rub a piece of abrasive paper along the surface of a piece to release the scented oil.

IDENTIFYING TIMBER

Carefully observing each of the five characteristics described above can help you to determine the species of timber used in the construction of a piece of furniture.

Having a collection of timber samples for comparison is another way of matching timbers for repair work.

Be aware, however, that many pieces of furniture will have been treated with a timber stain. Applying a stain to timber is a convenient way to even out the grain colour or to hide the use of other, less expensive species of timber in some parts.

You should check for signs of stain application on the underside of timber pieces before you start the repair process.

MAKING FURNITURE

Eighteenth, nineteenth and early twentieth century cabinet makers generally used solid timber when constructing furniture.

HINT

A piece of new timber that is the same species as a piece of old timber will not be a perfect colour match.

The reason for this is that timber oxidises with age and the natural pigments within it change over time. The pigments also react to sunlight and timber generally gets darker with age.

A useful technique for artificially ageing new timber is to machine and sand the timber as it is to be finished, then place the piece in the sun and leave it there for a few days. While this technique will not result in a perfect colour match, it speeds the ageing process and works particularly well for timbers that are light in colour.

Veneers were sometimes used as decoration, to hide timbers that were of inferior quality or to change the direction of the grain.

Framing techniques were used to join the separate parts of a piece together. In old pieces, dowel, mortise and tenon and dovetail joints are common.

Modern furniture pieces are often made of flat-panelled wood products such as veneered particle board and plywood. Modern construction techniques involve the use of many engineered jointing devices to hold components together while adhesives set.

Advances in drilling technology have increased the use of screws and the range of furniture fittings that are available. This, in turn, has influenced the design of contemporary furniture.

FINISHING TECHNIQUES

In the eighteenth and nineteenth centuries, furniture was often highly polished using a technique called 'French polishing'. Wax or oil polish was used as an alternative to this polishing method.

These surface finishes were not very resilient and were marked easily, so they required constant retouching to keep them looking good.

A sprayed finish of lacquer, which was unavailable prior to the twentieth century because it requires advanced technology to produce, is the most common finish used on modern furniture.

Repairing dents and scratches

There are a number of different methods of repairing blemishes to timber surfaces. The method used depends upon the blemish, its location and the type of material that has been damaged.

ASSESSING THE DAMAGE

Before choosing a method of repair, you need to assess the damage to the timber by looking carefully at the surface and the surrounding areas to see if any of the surface fibres have been fractured.

A fine, relatively deep crack across the fibres means that the timber has been fractured. These cracks need to be filled. Small dents and scratches in unfractured timber can often be simply steamed out or sanded back.

Rust stains on timber surfaces can be removed by brushing the stain with oxalic acid, and bubbles in veneered timber can be smoothed out by slicing the veneer surface and gluing the area down.

SMALL DENTS AND SCRATCHES

• To remove a dent from an unfinished solid timber surface, place a wet rag over the damaged area and press a hot iron down against the rag. Make sure that the rag covers the entire area of the dent. Wait a few seconds, then remove the iron and the cloth. Let the area dry then check it to see if the dent has been removed. You may need to apply the wet rag and iron a few times to remove the entire dent. The iron's steam penetrates the compressed surface fibres of the timber, causing them to swell back to their original state, removing the dent. When the dent has been removed, sand the surface of the timber.

• Dents in veneered particle board can be steamed out in the same way. However, the veneer is only about 1 mm thick, so be careful when sanding not to expose the particle board substrate below.

• Dents and bruises can also simply be sanded out using abrasive paper or scraped flat using a cabinet scraper. You should take care, however, not to sand only around the immediate area of the dent. This will cause a deeper indentation which is often more noticeable on a

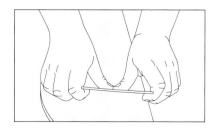

Some small dents can be removed simply by smoothing the surface of the dented area with a scraper.

The timber top of this wash stand has a fracture along its width, which will need to be filled. The small dents can be steamed and sanded out.

flat surface than a little filler. When sanding, rub the abrasive paper or the scraper over a broad area and don't be tempted to use the heel or the toe of a sanding machine. Always sand or scrape timber in the same direction as the grain.

• An option for unfinished timbers is to place a small amount of methylated spirits over the area to be raised. Allow the methylated spirits a few moments to soak into the timber, then set the methylated spirits alight. Be careful, however, when using this method of repair. In particular, do not use too much methylated spirits, as this can scorch the surface and you will then have to sand the scorch mark out.

SMALL DENTS IN A PIECE WITH A MODERN LACQUERED FINISH
It is very difficult to remove a dent in a timber surface with a modern lacquered finish without damaging the surface finish. There is, however, one method you can try. If the surface finish is intact, make pin holes through the lacquer into the timber, then apply a damp rag to the surface and press the rag gently with a warm iron for short periods. Make sure the iron is not too hot; it should be set on low to medium heat. Use cotton cloth and do not apply undue pressure to the cloth with the iron.

A few white patches may form under the lacquer as a result of using this technique. These can be removed quite easily by wiping with a cloth dampened with a mixture composed of equal parts of lacquer thinner and turpentine.

FRACTURES

When a dent or hole is too deep or large to steam out and the surrounding timber has been fractured the area should be filled. There are a number of products that can be used.

WOOD PUTTY

The first product is wood putty. There are two sorts: water-based and turpentine-based. Both of these types are available in a range of popular timber colours.

The advantage of using water-based putty is that it can be coloured to match a timber's hue with the use powdered pigments. These are available from shops that stock French polishing products. Coloured pigments can be added to wet putty or mixed with water and painted onto dry putty. Pigments of different colours can be mixed together to create a close colour match.

Before applying putty, make sure the hole or dent that you want to fill is free from dust. Use a putty knife or a similar object to push the putty well into the hole.

If the hole is shallow, use a pin to make a number of small holes in the dent to help anchor the putty in the hole. Fill the hole to above the level of the surface. Allow the putty plenty of time to dry then sand the putty

Powdered pigments in a selection of colours; from top, brown, yellow, green and orange.

back to the level of the surface. You may need to apply a second layer of the putty, as certain brands have a tendency to sink a little as they dry.

If you intend to add coloured pigments, start by using a light base colour and adding darker colours a little at a time until you get the right hue. Bear in mind that the colour of the wet putty will closely match the colour of the filler after a clear finish is applied.

Turpentine-based wood fillers can be tinted by adding a little oil-based stain. Use an eye dropper and add the stain one drop at a time, as the colour tends to be quite strong.

PLASTIC FILLERS

For dents that cannot be filled with standard timber putty, you can use a plastic filler. This usually comes as a two-part mixture, one part filler and the other hardener.

Plastic fillers set hard and can generally be filed, drilled and screwed, so they are useful for filling large holes, such as holes left by knots. Plastic filler is also the best filler for a bruise on a sharp edge.

Read the manufacturer's instructions before mixing and only mix up the amount you need for the job. The dent should be filled and left to dry before you sand or file it flush with the surface.

Plastic fillers can be coloured using either pigments or stains. Add the colouring before adding the hardener.

As plastic fillers do not soak up stain after they have set, colouring them later can be difficult. It's best to get the colour right while the filler is wet. In view of this, use a filler that has a white hardener. If you intend to use a car body filler, check the hardener, as most types have a coloured hardener.

WAX FILLERS

Wax fillers are available in stick form in a range of timber colours suitable for most repairs. They can be used on scratches and dents in both finished and unfinished surfaces and are extremely useful on pre-finished melamine boards, as they can be polished over and touched up after finishing and also can be blended with powdered pigments to create many different shades of colour.

To blend a wax stick with a powdered pigment, put the wax stick in a jar and put the jar inside a saucepan filled with water. Place the saucepan on the stove and bring the water to the boil—this will melt the wax. Add the powdered pigment, stir until thoroughly blended and allow the mixture to cool.

To apply the wax, rub it over the damaged area until a coating has been applied. With a clean putty knife, remove the excess.

Give the area a final finish with an appropriate abrasive. Use 180- to 320-grit paper for bare timber or

Wax sticks come in a range of colours, matching those of popular timbers.

0000 grade steel wool for polished timber surfaces.

Alternatively, use the blade of a putty knife that has been warmed by your hand to push the wax into the hole or scratch. This method has the advantage of being the least messy and doesn't leave as much residue.

You could also melt a couple of drops of wax into the dent or scratch using a flame. However, the carbon residue from the flame has a tendency to mix with the wax and darken its colour.

REMOVING RUST STAINS

Rust marks, which are generally caused by ageing nails and screws, can be removed from timber surfaces by applying a solution of oxalic acid and water. Oxalic acid can be ordered from specialty furniture supply shops, pharmacies and some hardware stores.

A few grams of oxalic acid is generally all that is needed for each job. Be sparing with the acid, as it tends to bleach timber. If light bleach patches appear on the timber surface, disguise them by applying a mild

---

EQUIPMENT

- 20 g oxalic acid
- Water
- Abrasive paper: Fine grade
- Pencil brush

---

solution of the acid to the entire timber surface.

1 Mix approximately 20 g of oxalic acid in about 100 ml of water. This will generally be enough to remove rust stains from a number of pieces of furniture.

2 Apply the mixture to each stain with a pencil brush and then allow to dry. When the mixture on each stain is dry, brush away the remaining acid crystals and sand each spot carefully with a fine-grade abrasive paper.

3 If the rust stain has not disappeared, repeat the procedure a second time. A maximum of three attempts should see it eliminated.

REPAIRING BUBBLED VENEER

Veneer that has lifted, causing bubbles under the surface, is common on old pieces. Bubbled veneer can be fixed easily and with little equipment. Either of two techniques can be used to fix the problem, depending on the sort of adhesive that has been used to glue down the veneer.

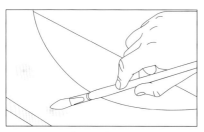

2 Paint oxalic acid mixture on each rust stain with a pencil brush. Brush away remaining crystals when dry.

VENEER GLUED DOWN WITH PVA ADHESIVE

1 With a utility knife, make a slit along the grain of the wood right across the bubble.

EQUIPMENT
• PVA adhesive
• Rag
• Block of scrap timber
• Utility knife or craft blade
• Large-needled syringe
• Quick-action cramp or heavy object

2 Fill a syringe with a large needle with PVA adhesive and slowly inject the adhesive into the slit in the bubble. Press the bubbled veneer down carefully with your fingers and remove the excess adhesive with a wet rag.

3 Place paper over the surface of the veneer. Put a block of scrap wood on top of the paper and then put pressure on the veneer surface by using a quick-action cramp. Alternatively, place a heavy object,

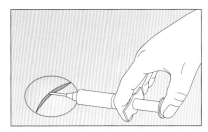

2 Fill a large-needled syringe with PVA adhesive and inject the adhesive into the bubble in the veneer.

such as a large telephone book, on the block.

VENEER GLUED DOWN WITH ANIMAL ADHESIVE

Animal adhesive was often used to glue down veneer on furniture constructed in the eighteenth and nineteenth centuries. To repair bubbled veneer glued with this type of adhesive, use the technique below.

EQUIPMENT
• Kitchen tongs
• Quick-action cramp
• Block of medium density fibreboard

1 Clean the finish from the surface of the area to be repaired.

2 Heat a block of medium density fibreboard (MDF) in a microwave or in a conventional oven to between very warm and hot. Undertake this carefully so that you do not set the block of MDF on fire.

3 Place the block in position over the bubble using kitchen tongs. Cramp the block down using a quick-release cramp, to put pressure on the surface.

4 Leave the cramp fixed in position until the block of MDF has cooled completely. The block's heat will cause the old adhesive to melt, and the adhesive will harden and re-grip the veneer as it cools.

Touching up blemishes

Even the simplest repair to a piece of furniture can result in the surface finish needing to be retouched. The first step to touching up a finish is to identify the type of finish used, then you can use the appropriate method of repair.

IDENTIFYING THE FINISH

The table below lists a few of the surface treatments that you can encounter and liquids that can be used to soften and identify them. Start testing the finish by applying a little methylated spirits in an area that is not noticeable. If the surface starts to get sticky, it will be French polish. If it is a nitro-cellulose lacquer, there will be little reaction. If it is a polyester, the surface will turn a milky white.

TOUCHING UP

When you have identified the surface treatment, mix a little stain with the correct finish medium and use a pencil brush to touch up the area. Make strokes in the direction of the grain to paint on a grain pattern. If the species of timber is knotty, such as radiata pine or oregon, you could try painting a replica knot over the damaged area.

If the repair you have made to the area is still noticeable, mix a little

SURFACE TREATMENT	SOFTENING TREATMENT/ FINISHING MEDIUM
French polish or shellac. Mainly used on antiques and pieces made prior to 1930.	Methylated spirits. A little paraffin oil dabbed on the pad containing the methylated spirits will reduce the risk of damaging the surface.
Nitro-cellulose lacquer. The most common finish used on contemporary furniture; it has been used since the 1960s.	Lacquer thinner mixed with an equal amount of turpentine.
Polyurethane. A recent addition to surface finishes, it is a two-pack paint which is extremely glossy as well as hard.	Special thinners and paint strippers. Polyurethane is very hard to touch up and should only be stripped and repainted by experts, as the finish must be perfectly flat.

pigment or stain with the finishing medium and apply it to the area with a pencil brush.

To restore an entire surface, clean the surface with warm soapy water, then rub it down with a pad of 0000 steel wool. When the surface has dried, apply the finish again.

FRENCH POLISH

1 To apply French polish to a surface, cover a pad of cotton wool with cotton cloth.

2 Dip the pad in a light mix of polish, then squeeze to remove most of the polish (the squeezed dry pad is known as a 'dry rubber'). Work the rubber in the direction of the grain, overlapping each stroke with the one before. Don't work in the same spot for too long, as the layers below it will soften and be 'dragged off'.

EQUIPMENT

- French polish
- Good quality cotton cloth
- Cotton wool
- Methylated spirits
- Burnishing cream

---

3 Gradually thin down the mix of French polish with methyated spirits and continue adding layers to the surface until you are satisfied with the finish.

4 Using burnishing cream, shine up the surface.

LACQUERS

1 Lightly scour the nitro-cellulose lacquer surface with steel wool.

EQUIPMENT

- Steel wool: 0000 grade
- Turpentine
- Lacquer thinner
- Good-quality cotton cloth
- Cotton wool

---

2 Rub the surface using a mixture of turpentine and lacquer thinner following the same padding technique as for French polish.

POLYURETHANE

1 To touch up a small area, sand the area with wet, then dry, abrasive paper, to remove surface scratches. Then rub it with the steel wool.

EQUIPMENT

- Abrasive paper: 800–1200 grit
- Steel wool: 0000 grade
- Cutting compound
- Lambs wool buffing pad
- Variable speed power drill

---

2 Use a cutting compound and the buffing pad attached to a power drill set on low speed to bring the gloss level up to that of the original. Cutting compound that is produced especially for cars is a good polish to use to restore polyurethane surfaces that are scuffed.

Restoring an occasional table

This triangular occasional table needed a bit of reconstruction work. A corner had broken off and needed to be replaced. Sections of veneer were also missing from its legs.

BROKEN CORNER

The most time-consuming repair—the reconstruction of the corner of the table top—was tackled first. As the repair was made to the table while it was standing upright, form work was prepared to hold the material chosen for the new corner in place.

Panel pins were inserted into the plywood substrata and a piece of stiff cardboard in the shape of the missing corner taped to the broken end. A plastic filler and hardener mixture was then pressed into place around the form work. When the putty had dried completely, the corner was filed and sanded to shape and edging tape was applied to the edges using a hot iron.

MISSING VENEER

The second repair was to the sections of missing veneer on the bottoms of the table's legs and around the new corner. The edges of the surrounding veneer were sliced away and the waste removed. Next, veneer edge tape with hot-melt adhesive backing was attached to the missing sections by applying the heat from an iron.

A little putty with a colour matching that of the original veneer surface was forced into the cracks between the new and the old veneer and the surface smoothed level. Finally, to shine up the surface, two coats of lacquer were applied to the repaired areas.

The new corner of the table matches the original two corners nicely and it is difficult to see that the repair has even been made. The new sections of veneer blend in beautifully with the original veneer surface too.

The sharp corners were a feature of the occasional table, so repairing the damaged one was essential.

There is now no sign that a section of the corner was missing, thanks to a thorough repair job. The new strips of veneer on the legs and around the corner are a precise match for the original veneer.

Repairing damaged corners

One corner of this small triangular table had been broken off and needed to be repaired. The table top's substrate is plywood.

METHOD

The broken shape was rebuilt using a two-part plastic putty. When mixed together this has a slightly runny consistency that is good for moulding shapes. Form work was constructed to hold the mixture in place while the resin set. As an alternative to the plastic putty, you could use a two-part epoxy resin putty. Using epoxy resin putty will save you the trouble of constructing form work.

1 If using plastic putty, snip the heads off two panel pins and insert them into the end of the corner for support. Tape a piece of stiff cardboard in the shape of the corner to the edges to prevent the putty spilling out. Smear soap or wax on the inside of the cardboard piece so that the cardboard will come away from the set putty easily.

2 Mix the amount of plastic putty required following the instructions supplied. Press the putty into place on the pins and mould it to the shape required. Mix some powdered pigment of a matching colour to the original surface with the plastic putty before adding the hardener. If using a two-part epoxy resin putty, mix an equal amount of each part together to form a stiff putty and simply mould it to the shape required. There is no need to add powered pigment to the epoxy resin putty as veneer is to be attached to it instead.

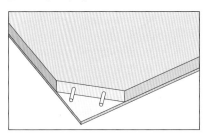

1 Insert a couple of panel pins into the end of the damaged corner so that you can rebuild it.

3 When the putty has set, reshape the corner to match the original, using files, abrasive paper and chisels.

The plywood substrate of the table's corner is clearly visible, spoiling its appearance.

The clean, sharp lines of the corner are in evidence again when it has been repaired.

4 You can veneer over the hardened plastic putty or apply a wood stain. If using epoxy resin putty, place a piece of veneer that matches that of the rest of the table over the putty.

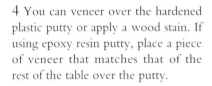

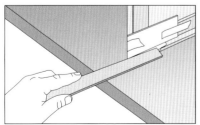

3 When the putty has set, reshape the corner to match the original using files, abrasive paper and chisels.

SLIGHT DAMAGE

Minor damage to corners with a plywood substrate can be repaired by carefully separating the layers. Using abrasive paper, push a small amount of epoxy resin adhesive between the layers and cramp the corner.

Epoxy resin adhesive sets harder than other types of adhesive and will restore the integrity of the timber. Cover the repaired corner with veneer tape backed with adhesive.

Revamping a writing box

This box was in desperate need of attention. The top of the box was fractured, sections of brass inlay were coming loose, the lid's hinges were missing and the leather writing slope was split.

REPAIRING THE FRACTURE

The first repair was to the fracture in the veneer top. Plastic putty was forced into the split, then pieces of timber were cramped to the split on the inside and outside faces of the lid while the putty hardened. When the putty had set, the excess was sanded off and a groove routed around the split to remove the veneer. A strip of new veneer was cramped in place and the area sanded and polished.

MENDING THE INLAY

The next task was to repair the damaged inlay sections. The

At first glance, the writing box looked beyond repair, but the damage, while extensive, was quite easily fixed.

damaged brass inlay was removed by holding a heated iron to it to soften the adhesive, then lifted away with a chisel. Epoxy resin adhesive was spread in the grooves and new brass cramped and secured in place until the adhesive had set. When the adhesive had dried, the brass strips were sanded flush, then the surface of the brass was given a final polishing.

The leather on the writing slope was damaged when the hinges broke, and it also needed replacing. Vinyl was used as a substitute, as leather was found to be too expensive. When the leather had been removed, the vinyl piece was sprayed with contact adhesive and slowly brought into contract with the slope.

FINISHING

Finally, the hinges for the lid were replaced. It wasn't possible to obtain new hinges the same size as the originals—those that were found were shorter and narrower. These were too small for the hinge recesses, so the area around each hinge recess was cut away and filled with solid timber to make a base for the new hinge. The box's finish was given a final touch up. The result of all the repair work is that the box looks superb.

The repaired writing box is almost unrecognisable. The box's decorative brass inlay has been replaced, enhancing its charm, and the natural beauty of the wood has been highlighted by touching up the surface finish.

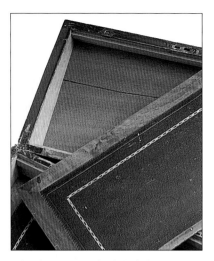

The damage to the lid of this writing slope was quite severe; there was a split through both sides.

The repaired split is visible on the lid's underside but on the outside face it is covered with new veneer.

Repairing splits in veneer

Splits in veneer surfaces are easily repaired by filling the fissures and covering them with new sections of veneer.

METHOD

1 Mix a batch of plastic filler and, with a putty knife, force it into the split in the veneer. Cramp pieces of

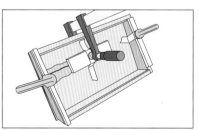

1 Cramp timber pieces along the length of the split, on the inside as well as the outside surface of the lid.

waxed timber the entire length of the split on both the inside and outside faces of the lid to keep both sides of the lid flush while the plastic filler hardens.

2 Remove the cramps and sand the plastic filler on the inside of the lid flush with the lid's face. Set a fence on both sides of the router to rout a groove to remove the veneer from around the split. The edges of the groove should be parallel with the edges of the box. Set the depth of the cutter to slightly less than the

EQUIPMENT

- Veneer sheet
- PVA adhesive; rags
- Abrasive paper
- Masking tape
- Plastic wood filler
- Newspaper
- Wax
- Adjustable cramps; G-cramps; quick-action cramps
- Utility knife
- Putty knife
- Electric router
- Router bit: grooving
- Cabinet scraper
- Sanding cork
- Steel straight edge
- Smoothing plane

between two straight edges and hold firmly together. There should be 1 to 2 mm of veneer showing between the straight edges. Plane a straight edge on the piece of veneer. Test the fit of the edge against the edge of the groove. Smooth the edge of the veneer with abrasive paper wrapped around a sanding cork. Turn the veneer around and plane the opposite edge until the piece fits neatly into the groove.

4 Spread adhesive in the groove and on the back of the veneer and wipe off the excess. Hold the veneer in place with masking tape. Lay newspaper over the veneer and place a piece of timber longer than the lid over the paper. Place another piece on the inside of the lid. Apply quick-action cramps and leave overnight.

thickness of the new veneer. Rout the groove in the box's veneer.

3 With a utility knife and a straight edge, cut a strip of new veneer slightly wider than the groove in the lid's outside face. Place the strip

5 Remove the cramps and trim the excess veneer from the ends with a utility knife. Remove the newspaper and masking tape, then use a scraper to flush the veneer off with the original surface. Sand and polish the veneer.

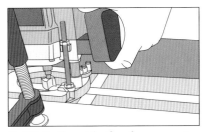

2 With the aid of a fence, rout a groove in the box's veneer to remove the veneer from around the split.

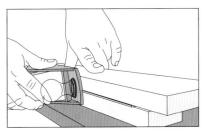

3 Place a smoothing plane on its side and plane a straight edge on the piece of veneer.

Most of the brass inlay strips on this writing box were damaged.

The new brass was obtained from a sheet metal supplier.

Replacing missing inlay

It is essential when repairing inlay that you use the right material. The method described for brass can also be used for veneer inlay.

METHOD

1 Carefully remove the inlay that remains by applying some heat to the strip with an iron to make the adhesive below soften and release the strip. Lift the strip, and any excess veneer, away with a chisel.

2 Ask your supplier to guillotine the new inlay to the correct width. Hold the edge of the strip of inlay straight against the edge of the groove in the furniture piece and, using a utility knife, slice along the edges of the new inlay through the veneer on either side of the groove. This will ensure that the groove will be wide enough to accept the inlay.

3 Mix a little epoxy resin adhesive and spread it in the groove using a putty knife. Spread the adhesive

thinly over the entire area. Place the new brass strip in the groove. Apply masking tape to it to prevent it from moving while it is cramped in place. Put some newspaper on the strip, a block of wood only as wide or slightly narrower than the brass strip on top, then cramp the strip in place to secure it.

4 When the adhesive has set completely, remove the cramps and

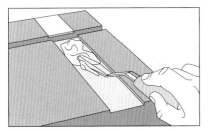

3 Place epoxy resin in the groove using a putty knife, spreading it thinly over the whole area.

use a chisel to remove any large lumps of epoxy resin that have leaked out.

5 Sand the surface flush, working in the direction of the timber grain. Take care not to sand through the veneer. The sanding will scratch the strips of brass but the surface of the brass can be restored later with careful sanding and polishing. Trim the overhang at each end with a pair of tin snips and file the ends back flush with the edge of the box with a mill saw file. Follow the procedure described above to clean back and glue any remaining strips of inlay neatly in position.

SUBSTITUTE MATERIALS

When restoring an antique piece, it's important to consider the impact replacement materials will have on the appearance and value of the piece, as well as the way it functions. For example, the leather inlay on the writing slope of this box was damaged badly when the hinges broke and it needed replacing. Vinyl was used as a substitute.

Leather would have been the most appropriate material to use as a replacement, but it is expensive, so vinyl, which is cheaper, was chosen instead. Another advantage of using vinyl is that it is easy to remove, so it can be replaced with leather when finances permit.

Reconstructing a chair

A forlorn object when discovered, this chair was missing a number of essential parts, including its seat. The leather inlay was also tattered.

REPLACING THE MISSING AND BROKEN PARTS

Before the chair was upholstered, the missing sections were replaced. A rubber mallet and timber block were used to break most of the joints of the chair apart. The corner blocks from the main seating area were removed with a hammer and chisel. The polish was then stripped off all of the parts to make it easier to identify the timber needed for the replacement pieces.

A new seat panel was constructed by tracing the seat's frame onto a piece of 18 mm particle board. The edges of the seat panel were rounded over to prevent them damaging the upholstery. The shape was then traced onto and cut from a piece of foam and the foam glued to the particle board. Small holes drilled though the seat panel allowed the foam to 'breathe'.

A piece big enough to replace the broken carved top rail was cut from new timber and glued and cramped in place. A cardboard template was made of the remaining top rail and this was flipped over and traced onto the new piece with a pencil. The new top rail was shaped by cutting along the pencil lines with a coping saw. Another rail missing from the back of the chair was cut and shaped in the same manner.

REPAIRING THE INLAY

Each part of the chair was sanded then the chair was reassembled and sent to an upholsterer to lay new leather. When the chair was returned, three coats of lacquer were applied. The result is an occasional chair that looks as good as new.

Despite its missing parts, the basic structure of the chair was sound, making it a suitable piece for repair.

The beauty of the chair's timber as well as its elegant lines and attractive leather inlay sections made the effort to replace parts and strip and retouch its finish all the more worthwhile.

The back of this chair was very unsteady as part of the curved top rail and a slat was missing.

The oak piece used to make the missing section was a good colour match and needed no retouching.

Replacing parts of a chair

This oak chair had a piece missing from its carved top rail, as well as a slat missing from the back. The top of the chair was dismantled so that the parts could be replaced.

DISMANTLING THE BACK OF THE CHAIR

1 Use a rubber mallet and a block of timber to break the joints of the back of the chair apart. Do this very carefully to avoid breaking timber and dowels.

2 Strip the polish or paint off the parts. If there is only a thin layer of polish or paint and the parts are

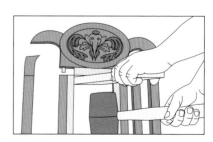

1 Using a rubber mallet and a block of timber, carefully break the joints at the back of the chair apart.

roughly square, you can use a belt sander with 100-grit sanding belt, otherwise apply paint stripper.

3 Use a wide bevelled-edge chisel to prepare a straight, square surface where the surface is broken and the top rail and slat on the chair back are missing. Use a square to check that the surface is square to the original face and flat.

REPLACING THE TOP RAIL

4 Cut a piece of new timber big enough to form the part (in this case, the missing section of the curved top rail; the curve at the top was left in place but the whole lower section was replaced). When joining pieces of long-grain timber, it is best to use a scarf joint (see the box on page 30). The joint will then be not as obvious. Use a sliding bevel to match the angles on both parts of the joint. Square the edges and plane the scarf joint if required.

5 Apply a small amount of adhesive to each of the faces of the joint and

---

EQUIPMENT

- Timber for repairs
- Urea-formaldehyde resin adhesive
- 100- to 120-grit abrasive belts
- Cardboard
- Slot- or cross-head screwdriver
- Hammer
- Rubber mallet
- 25 mm chisel
- Belt sander or paint stripper
- Flat-bottom spokeshave
- Cramps
- Utility knife
- Jigsaw or coping saw
- Half-round wood rasp
- Scissors
- Smoothing plane
- Cabinet scraper
- Sanding cork
- Sliding bevel (optional)

---

cramp the new piece of timber in place. Leave the two timber parts cramped together overnight to allow the adhesive enough time to dry.

HINT

If a joint won't break apart easily, flood it with water. This will soften the adhesive, making it easier to take the joint apart. This technique should only be used on solid timber joints, however, as water degrades manufactured boards.

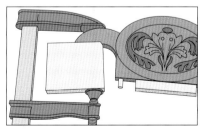

5 Apply adhesive to the faces of the joint and cramp the new piece of timber in place.

SCARF JOINTS

A scarf joint joins timber end to end with bevels cut on the end of each piece of timber so that uniform thickness is maintained.

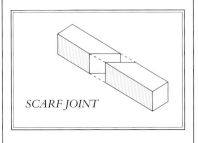

SCARF JOINT

REPLACING DOWELS

The dowel connecting two sections of a joint sometimes breaks when a joint is taken apart. If this happens, you will need to replace the dowel. To do this, use a power drill with a twist bit attached or a hand drill with an auger bit attached to remove the piece of dowel that remains and redrill the holes of the joint. Make sure the drill bit has a long centre point and clean cutting spurs. Countersink the top of the dowel holes to remove any fibres. Apply adhesive to the holes and hammer in a new dowel. Then cramp the joint together.

6 On a piece of cardboard, trace around the back of the unbroken curved top rail with a pencil to make a template. Make the outline of the new piece a little bigger than the part you are tracing to enable you to clean up and fit the new top rail. Cut out the template and flip it over.

7 Place the template on the back of the broken curved top rail and trace around it with a pencil. Use a jigsaw or a coping saw to cut the required shape. File back to the

pencil lines using a flat-bottom spokeshave for the external curves and a half-round or rat-tail wood rasp for the internal curves.

MAKING THE SLAT
8 Place the chair's remaining slat on the new piece of timber, and trace around it with a pencil. Make the outline a little longer than the

7 Place the template on the back of the broken curved top rail and trace around it with a pencil.

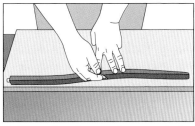

8 Place the slat on the new timber and trace around it with a pencil, making the outline a little longer.

original slat so that the piece can be cleaned up and fitted.

9 Cramp the timber to a suitable work surface, such as a bench or table, and cut along the pencil outline with a jigsaw or coping saw. Use a flat-bottom spokeshave or a smoothing plane to clean up the external (convex) curves of the sawn surface, and a belt sander to clean up the shallow internal (concave) curves of the surface.

REASSEMBLING AND FINISHING

10 Give each part of the back of the chair a thorough sanding with 180-grit abrasive paper. Then reassemble the back of the chair and glue and cramp the joints together. Fit the slats and the back-rest frame before placing the top rail in position. Insert

---

HINT

It is easier to identify and match timber for replacement parts if you strip a piece of timber furniture before repairing it.

Take a part that has been stripped to a timber yard and ask a salesperson to help you identify the species of timber and select a replacement piece from the range available for that species. Take a smoothing plane with you, as most of the stock will be rough-sawn and it is hard to judge colour and grain pattern from a rough-sawn piece.

UREA FORMALDEHYDE RESIN

Using the correct adhesive is important when repairing chairs, as they are subjected to a lot of stress when in use. Urea formaldehyde resin adhesive, a two-part adhesive that sets hard and has little creep, unlike PVA adhesive, was used for this chair. 'Creep', or 'plasticity', is the tendency to move.

Urea formaldehyde comes generally as a white resin with a brown powder hardener. Follow the manufacturer's instructions and mix just enough together to do the job, as the adhesive will start to set in about 20 to 30 minutes, depending on the amount of hardener used and the prevailing weather conditions. Don't use too much hardener, as this causes the adhesive to crystallise, making it brittle.

---

any necessary new dowels (see the box on page 30). Use a rubber mallet and protective block to bring the components together. Wipe off any excess adhesive with a wet rag before it sets. The force exerted by the cramps should just be enough to close the joints tight. Leave the chair frames in the cramps overnight so that the adhesive has time to dry and the joints gain sufficient strength. When the adhesive is dry, shape the head rail, using a spokeshave and wood rasp, where it meets the leg.

Rejuvenating a wash stand

When this wash stand was brought in for repair it was finished with a dismal brown paint. A number of its parts also needed to be replaced.

REMOVING THE FINISH

Paint stripper was used to remove the brown finish. The attractive timber hidden under the paint was identified as kauri pine. This wood was commonly used to make furniture in the Victorian era. Scratches and dents on the top of the stand were steamed out then sanded smooth.

MAKING NEW PARTS

Replacement pieces were then made for the broken apron on the top and for a shelf that was attached to the lower part of the legs. To do this, templates of the pieces were made by tracing around remaining similar parts. For the broken apron piece, this was the opposite apron; for the shelf, it was the back board. The templates were traced onto pieces of kauri pine and the parts cut out and secured into position.

FITTING NEW TURNED PIECES TO THE LEGS

The ends of the legs of the stand had been removed and replaced with tapered turnings in the 1960s. These unattractive sections were removed and replaced with turned sections matching those of the original legs. Photographs were taken of similar wash stand legs found at antique stores and these were given to a wood turner to use as reference. The unattractive tapered turnings were cut off and the new sections attached by drilling holes in the new pieces and the ends of the legs and inserting dowels. The repairs now complete, the washstand was restored to its original condition.

An unattractive brown finish completely disguised the wash stand's beautiful natural timber.

The appearance of the wash stand was vastly improved with the replacement of the side apron, bottom shelf and lower sections of the legs, and by stripping away the paint and applying a natural finish.

Replacing a shaped component

The top edge of a side apron on this wash stand had been damaged and the piece needed replacing. The apron's bottom edge was bevelled so that it sat at the correct angle on top of the stand.

MATERIALS
• Timber (same species as piece)
• PVA adhesive
• 180- to 240-grit abrasive paper
• Masking tape

TOOLS
• Tenon saw and mitre box or mitre saw
• Flat-bottom spokeshave
• Quick-action cramps
• Utility knife
• Electric drill
• 1 mm drill bit
• Jigsaw or coping saw
• Half-round wood rasp
• Sliding bevel
• Smoothing plane
• Cabinet scraper
• Sanding cork
• Combination square

CUTTING THE REPLACEMENT PIECE

1 Remove the broken piece and the matching unbroken piece. Make a replacement piece for the broken component by tracing around the outline of the unbroken piece on a piece of new timber. Make the new piece a little longer than the unbroken piece to allow you to cut the mitre.

2 Cut out the shape of the replacement piece with a jigsaw or a coping saw. Plane a bevel on the bottom edge of the replacement piece so that it will sit at the correct angle on the top of the wash stand. To do this, use a sliding bevel to

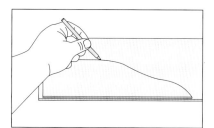

1 Trace around the outline of the remaining side apron piece on the new piece of timber.

4 Use a mitre box or vice and a tenon saw to cut the mitre on the new side apron piece.

On this wash stand, the top edge of a side apron had broken off, ruining the entire apron.

The new side apron was shaped to match the apron piece opposite it on the stand.

capture the angle of the bevel on the unbroken piece, then plane the bevel on the replacement piece to the same angle.

FORMING THE MITRES ON THE NEW PIECE

3 Mark the length of the original piece on the new piece, across the outside face. Mark the return mitre on the edge of the new piece, using a combination square.

4 Use a mitre box and tenon saw to the cut the mitre. You could use a vice and a tenon saw instead. Plane the mitre to the correct length using a smoothing plane.

ATTACHING THE NEW PIECE

5 Lay the pieces out on a bench with the mitres aligned and use some masking tape to hold the joints together. Turn the assembly over, place a little adhesive in the joint and fold the assembly up to form the corners. Use a little masking tape to hold the corners in position. Check that they are square.

6 Let the adhesive dry overnight, then use a 1 mm drill bit to make pilot holes for 1.25 mm panel pins. Insert the pins into the joints to strengthen the assembly. Assemble the apron piece on the top.

Repairing splits in solid timber

Before repairing a break in solid timber, you should investigate the nature of the damage, determine its cause and work out the best possible repair so that the damage won't occur again.

REPAIRING A SPLIT

1 Using a chisel as a lever, carefully remove any pieces attached to the timber. Take care to avoid splitting any old timber. Remove any nails left in the frame with pincers or a scraper. Pull any nails left in the panels through the underside of the timber. A nail punch can be used to punch the nails through the panel and out the underside. Choose a punch that is the same size or a little smaller than the head of the nail. Any evidence of chipping on the underside of the timber will be hidden from view when the piece is reattached to the frame.

2 If the joints are not broken, put epoxy resin adhesive in the splits. Hold each split open with a small timber wedge or a chisel, then apply the adhesive. Take care not to split the timber further. To fill a split that is very narrow, put a little adhesive on a piece of abrasive paper and insert the paper into the split, then remove the paper.

3 Cramp the splits together, applying pressure in two directions using quick-action cramps. Use cramping blocks to protect the timber and put

EQUIPMENT
● Abrasive paper: 180–240 grit
● Epoxy resin adhesive
● Waxed paper or newspaper
● Finish of choice
● 25 mm chisel
● Hammer
● Pincers or cabinet scraper
● Quick-action cramps
● Nail punch
● Paint brush or spray gun

waxed paper or newspaper between the blocks and the timber to prevent the blocks from being glued to the timber.

FINISHING

4 Give the furniture piece a final sand all over with 180- to 240-grit abrasive paper, then apply a finish of your choice. A modern finish of water-based acrylic lacquer was applied to the blanket box in the photograph above. The handles of this blanket box were removed and sprayed with a black gloss paint from a pressure pack and reattached to the box when the finish had completely dried.

The solid timber at the back of the lid of this box was split in two and was desperately in need of repair.

The repair to the lid is visible but attaching a chain to the lid's inside will ensure the split won't reoccur.

SECURING A LID

The break in timbers in this blanket box occurred because the lid was allowed to drop back too far, putting strain on the timber and the joints. To prevent the split recurring, the timber around the break needs to be reinforced.

1 Remove the lid. Choose a timber for the stiffening rails that matches the species used for the box.

2 With a tenon saw, cut the stiffening rails to length. Glue and cramp the rails to the inside faces of the box and lid, adjacent the hinges.

3 Reattach the lid, replacing the hinges and screws, if necessary, and screw-fix a length of light chain to the inside of the lid and box to prevent the lid falling back. The chain should allow the lid to open so that it is nearly vertical. Do not allow the lid to open at a greater angle, as this could cause the joint to break.

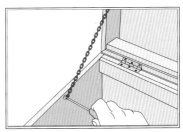

3 Screw-fix a small length of chain to the inside of the lid and box to prevent the lid falling back too far.

Repairing widening joints

Butt-glued joints in boards may eventually come apart even in well-constructed pieces of furniture. Some adhesives lose their strength over time and this, combined with timber shrinkage, occasionally causes a bond to break.

CHECKING THE JOINTS

1 The panel will be in two parts. Inspect the line of the joint to determine how the two parts are held together. The instructions here are for repairing butt-glued joints. The relatively new method of 'biscuit' or plate joiners can be used to re-join two pieces. Biscuit or plate joiners are elliptical pieces of beech timber measuring approximately 3 to 4 mm thick, which are designed to fit in a slot made by a portable machine. This method of joining is relatively quick and, if the biscuit-joining

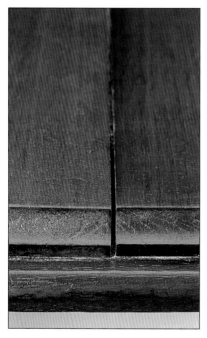

There was a noticeable gap in the two top pieces of this table where the joint was coming apart.

The table top was reassembled to remove the unsightly gap between the two pieces.

MATERIAL

- PVA adhesive
- Five No. 20 joining plates
- Rags
- Clamping blocks
- Masking tape

TOOLS

- Slot head or cross-head screwdriver
- Hammer
- 25 mm or wider chisel
- Two or three 1500 mm sash cramps
- Utility knife
- Plate or 'biscuit' joining machine or a dowelling jig and 8 mm dowels
- Electric drill
- Drill bit: 5 mm
- Smoothing plane
- Cabinet scraper
- Sanding cork

machine is operated correctly, more accurate than dowelling, particularly if the piece does not require re-polishing. Biscuit-joining machines are available for hire at many tool hire shops.

BUILT-UP EDGES

The tops of some tables have built-up edges. These sometimes need to be removed to make repairs to the table top. Built-up edges are often simply screwed and glued to the table top using standard countersunk screws and are not slot screwed, which allows some movement of the timber. To remove and reattach built-up edges fixed to a table using the slot screwed method, follow these steps:

1 Remove the screws from the built-up edges using a screwdriver. Insert a utility knife in the joint line between the two pieces of the top on both the top face and the underside to break the line of adhesive. This should prevent the built-up edges splitting when you remove them.

2 To prepare the built-up edges for attachment, elongate the screw holes in the table, particularly those screw holes running across the grain of the wood, to allow the wood to move.

3 On the face that is to be joined, use a smoothing plane to remove old adhesive and bits of wood from the surface so that the surface is flat and smooth. Make sure, however, that you don't inadvertently remove any of the polish from the built-up edge. To avoid removing polish from the built-up edge, place masking tape over the polished area and stop planing when you reach the line of tape.

4 Place the built-up edges on the top and screw them into place.

REMOVING PAINT FROM TURNED PARTS

It is extremely difficult to completely remove paint from the surface of turned parts, such as the legs on traditional tables. Even after a thorough sanding paint residue is often still evident in the crevices and on the end grain of table legs. The only way to completely remove paint or stain from turned timber is to have the part re-turned on a lathe to remove the top 1 or 2 mm of the timber.

Re-turning timber reduces the size of the turnings, however, and this may adversely change the lovely proportions of the original structure.

A less complete but safer method than re-turning the part affected is to use a stainless-steel wool scourer, a scraper and a scrubbing brush in combination with paint stripper to remove residue from places that are hard to reach.

JOINING THE BOARDS

2 Place the two panels to be joined face up on the work bench with the edges to be joined together and aligned. Mark the centre point of the pieces (the first joint mark).

3 Draw joint marks at 250 mm intervals. If you aren't polishing the piece later, draw the marks on pieces of masking tape taped to the panel instead of on the panel itself so you can remove the marks with the tape.

CUTTING A GROOVE IN THE CENTRE

4 Set the cutter (the small saw-like blade) the correct depth to cut a groove in the centre of the thickness of the boards. Check that the depth of the cut corresponds to the plate size you are using. (Biscuit plates come in three sizes: Nos 0, 10 and 20. For this project, No. 20 joining plates were used.)

5 Cut a few grooves on a piece of scrap timber to get used to the

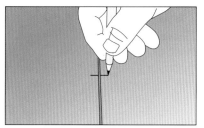

2 Mark the centre point of the pieces and then make joint marks at 250 mm intervals.

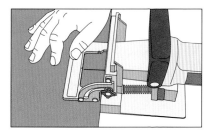

6 Align the centre mark of the first joint on one piece with that on the face plate of the biscuit joiner.

biscuit-joining machine before starting work on the panels.

6 Align the centre mark of the first joint on one piece with the centre mark on the face plate of the machine and make a cut. Then make the remaining cuts in that piece and make the cuts in the second piece.

INSERTING THE PLATES

7 Put adhesive on the face of the joints and in the grooves. Hammer the plates a little thinner, as the adhesive will make them swell.

8 Using one of the plates, push the adhesive into each of the grooves then, with a finger, spread the excess over the face of the biscuit joint. Wipe off any runs with a rag.

9 Insert the plates and bring the two pieces together using cramps. Make sure that the edges of the pieces are aligned before tightening the screws on the cramps.

10 With a damp rag, wipe off any adhesive that remains before it sets. Leave the panel in the cramps overnight to allow time for the adhesive to dry.

FINISHING

11 Check the panel for any damage and, if necessary, make repairs. Finally, re-attach the panel to the frame. Sand the area around the join in the boards and retouch the finish.

REPLACING EDGE STRIPS

This repair requires little equipment and is simple to do. All you need is edge tape, 120-grit abrasive paper, an electric iron, a sanding cork and a file.

1 Apply the hot iron to the existing tape to remove it.

2 Hold the new tape in position over the edge, with an even overhang on each side. Working from one end, place abrasive paper under the hot iron and use the heat to melt the tape's adhesive, gluing it down. Place a sanding cork behind the iron and push the tape down flat. Trim the ends of the tape with the file.

3 Lay the panel on a flat surface and, using a scissor action, remove the excess tape from the edges with the file. Using the sanding cork and the 120-grit abrasive paper, smooth the arris on the edge.

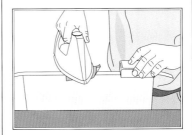

2 With abrasive paper between the edging tape and the iron, use a hot iron to melt the adhesive.

With the third leg missing from the pedestal, this occasional table did not stand upright without support.

The faces of the joint were cleaned up and the leg reattached, making the table functional again.

Repairing a broken pedestal

Occasionally, one lower leg on a table's pedestal snaps off. If the leg itself is sound, reattaching it is quite simple.

TOOLS
• 12 mm bevelled-edge chisel
• Quick-action cramps
• Sanding cork

MATERIALS
• 240-grit abrasive paper
• Epoxy resin adhesive
• Pigmented oil stain
• Spray lacquer
• 0000 grade steel wool
• Wood filler
• Mineral turpentine
• Fine pencil brush
• Masking tape

METHOD

1 Check to see if the leg and the joint are sound by putting the leg back into its original position. If the leg goes in quite easily, all that is needed is a repair to the joint.

REPAIRING THE PEDESTAL JOINT

2 To repair the leg's pedestal joint, clean up the faces of the joint, removing any old adhesive. Check the fit of the leg in the slot—it should go in smoothly and with minimal pressure. If it doesn't, use a fine bevelled-edge chisel to smooth the sides of the groove until the joint fits neatly.

3 Apply adhesive to the faces of the leg and the joint. The best adhesive to use for gluing the joint is epoxy resin. This will make the joint stronger than the timber—the result being that the joint will not break at this point again. Hold the leg in position with masking tape while you apply quick-action cramps. Clean away any adhesive that remains on the leg using a rag moistened with a little methylated spirits. Don't use a lacquer thinner to remove the excess adhesive. While effective, if the surface is lacquered a thinner may damage the finish, resulting in you needing to strip the surface and reapply the finish. Sand

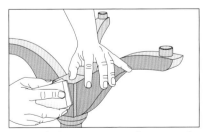

3 Sand the uneven surfaces on the table's pedestal flush using 240-grit abrasive paper.

TOUCHING UP LACQUER FINISHES

When buying a lacquer to touch up a section of a piece, bear in mind that there are several levels of gloss available. Choose one that matches the finish on the piece you want to retouch. You will probably need three coats of lacquer to get a good result.

If the new gloss stands out from the original or a staining process goes awry, be prepared to finish the entire piece again. Some blemishes can be disguised, however, by dipping a fine pencil brush in a mixture of stain and lacquer and painting on grain features. You should practise this disguise on a piece of scrap material first and use it sparingly.

---

any uneven surfaces on the pedestal flush using 240-grit abrasive paper. This will expose the timber below, so re-staining may be needed if the piece is lacquered. If this is the case, use a pigmented oil-based stain thinned with a little turpentine. Apply several coats over a few days to build up to the right shade gradually and obtain a good colour match.

FINISHING

4 If the piece is lacquered, spray on lacquer from an aerosol can to touch up the repaired area. If the piece is painted, you may be able to just touch up the area or you may need to strip the entire piece and paint it again.

Replacing broken fretwork

This little shelf had damaged fine fretwork, which needed to be replaced. The fretwork was attached to a curved edge, so bending plywood was used to construct the new piece.

REMOVING THE BROKEN FRETWORK

1 Study the fretwork's design to discover its centre, then remove it, remembering to save a large piece for tracing the design. Lever off the pieces carefully with a chisel and use a pair of pincers to remove any panel pins. Remove old adhesive with the chisel. Bending plywood, used for new fretwork that is to be attached to a curved edge, will bend more easily across than along the grain, so if you are using this type of plywood ensure that when you trace the pattern of the fretwork you orient it accordingly.

FINDING THE FRETWORK'S CENTRE

2 Measure the width of the fretwork. Use a pencil, tape and square to mark this on the new piece of plywood. Find the centre of the piece and square the centre line across it.

3 To find the centre of a curved edge, such as the edge the fretwork is attached to, run a length of string along the edge. Find the centre of the length of string, mark it and then mark the distance from the centre mark to the end of the length of string on the new piece. Mark the distance from the centre mark to the other end on the other half of the new piece.

TRACING THE PATTERN

4 Trace the pattern of the original fragment of fretwork onto the new piece of plywood. Keep tracing the

---

EQUIPMENT

- Piece of bending or other plywood
- PVA adhesive
- Wood putty knife
- Wood stain and spray lacquer or appropriate finish
- Length of string (optional)
- Piece of split cane with an 8–10 mm diameter
- Quick-action cramps or adjustable cramps
- Sanding cork
- Tenon saw or jigsaw
- Scroll saw or coping saw and spare blades
- Electric drill and appropriate size drill bit
- Utility knife
- Putty knife
- Hammer
- Pincers
- Chisel
- Tape measure; pencil; square

The damage to the middle section of the shelf's decorative fretwork was severe but not beyond repair.

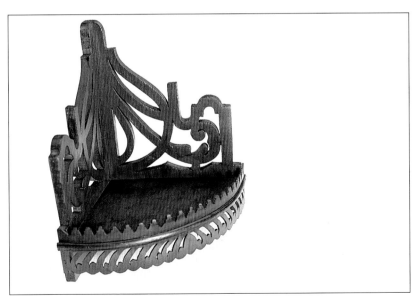

New fretwork was shaped from plywood and the piece was attached to the edge of the shelf and finished to match the remaining timber.

pattern until you reach the centre,
then turn the piece over and trace
the pattern's mirror image on the
other side of the centre line. Draw
any missing areas freehand.

CUTTING THE FRETWORK

5 Using a tenon saw, jigsaw or a
coping saw, cut the new piece roughly
to width, allowing a little extra for
waste, and make it a little longer to
allow for overhang at the ends.

6 Place a piece of plywood as
backing behind the fretwork piece to
prevent break out. Drill holes large
enough to accept the blade of the
coping saw at each place the
fretwork is to be pierced.

7 Set the piece in a vice so that the
pierced areas are accessible and insert
the blade of the coping saw through
the first hole. Then attach the frame
of the saw to the blade and cut out
the first piece. The blade of the
coping saw can be rotated 360
degrees, so it can cut in any
direction. If you haven't used this
type of saw before, you should
practise before cutting the fretwork.

8 Make all the cuts for the pierced
work. Then cut the top edge of the
fretwork and turn it over and cut the
bottom edge of the fretwork.

ATTACHING THE
FRETWORK

9 Align the centre mark on the
fretwork piece with the centre mark
on the shelf, nail a panel pin into the
fretwork at the centre mark and bend
the fretwork around the shelf all the
way to the ends.

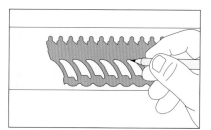

*4 On the new piece of plywood,
trace around the pattern of the
fretwork fragment.*

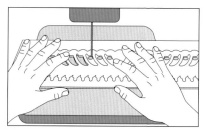

*7 Insert the blade of the saw through
the hole, then attach the frame and
cut the pierced shape.*

BAND SAWS

A band saw is a handy tool to have in the workshop. It can perform a range of sawing tasks and will help you to improve your productivity. Band saws are quite cheap when the number of jobs that they can perform is taken into consideration. Straight lines, curves and circles can all be tackled and some have a tilting bed that enables you to make compound angle cuts. The edge you receive is fairly rough but band saws are good for shaping timber and for removing large amounts of waste quickly.

REPLACING VENEER

If you want to replace a piece of veneer in from an edge, hold the piece of veneer firmly in place over the spot, making sure the grain is aligned accurately, and make an elongated eye-shaped cut through both layers of veneer. Remove the waste, glue the new piece in place and press firmly down with a sanding cork or scrap block. If the veneer sits proud, use a cabinet scraper to level it flush with the old surface. If this is the case, you should have stripped the entire surface of the top already so finish the top as you had planned.

10 Mark the length each side of the centre. Remove the panel pin and cut the piece to length.

11 Apply a little adhesive to the edge of the shelf. Align the end of the fretwork with the end of the shelf.

12 Insert two panel pins and apply a quick-action cramp at this point to

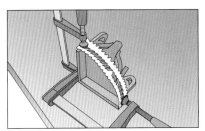

12 Bend and nail the fretwork around the shelf's curved edge and apply cramps to both ends.

hold the fretwork in place. Then bend and nail the fretwork around the curved edge. Make sure you fit the piece squarely to the edge. Cramp the opposite end and leave the assembly cramped while the adhesive dries.

FINISHING

13 Pin and glue a split cane bead over the nail heads in the fretwork. New split cane should be soaked for about 30 minutes in water to make it pliable. Then apply stain to the fretwork using a brush, and wipe off the excess.

14 Finally, spray the shelf with a couple of coats of clear lacquer from a pressure can, sanding lightly between coats.

Repairing a drawer

Like many drawers in old chests, the sides of this drawer were badly worn with use. They were also split in places and there were large gouges in the drawer runners.

REPAIRING THE SIDES OF THE DRAWER

To repair the drawer sides, the damaged timber must be removed. The sides are then re-attached using drawer slips. This procedure gives the drawers a wider bearing surface, which prevents them from wearing out rapidly and bridges faults in the drawer runners.

1 Place the drawer upside down and remove the drawer bottom from the drawer. With a tenon saw, cut directly behind the drawer front piece down to the top of the groove made for the side of the drawer.

2 With a jigsaw or panel saw, cut along the groove from the back of the drawer to the front and remove the bottom edge of the side of the drawer. Clean the remaining timber back to the old groove line at the front of the drawer using a 25 mm wide chisel. Then remove the remaining waste down to the groove line using a smoothing plane.

3 Turn to the back of the drawer front and measure the distance from the bottom of the drawer to the top of the groove. Install a 5 mm grooving bit in a router and cut a groove 7 mm deep along the face of

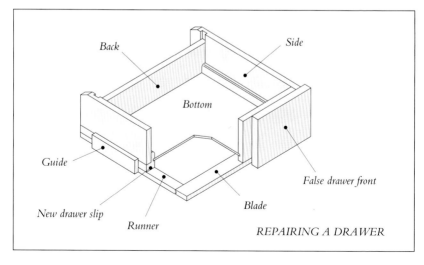

Back

Side

Bottom

Guide

New drawer slip

Runner

Blade

False drawer front

REPAIRING A DRAWER

The uneven bottom side edge of the drawer on top of the chest reveals its faults—worn sides and a loose bottom insert. The drawer runners were also worn.

To make the drawer functional again, its sides were reinforced, new runners were made and a false bottom was placed on top of the existing one. The drawer now slides easily open and closed.

EQUIPMENT
(REPAIRING THE SIDES)

- A piece of 41 x 25 mm timber, 2.4 m long for the drawer slip

- A piece of timber, a piece of 6 mm plywood or a piece of 6 mm medium density fibreboard for a new drawer bottom

- 5/8 in x 5 gauge countersunk screws or 20 mm flat-head nails

- PVA adhesive

- Smoothing plane

- 25 mm chisel

- Panel saw

- Tenon saw

- Jigsaw

- Four quick-action cramps

- Putty knife

- Hammer

---

the piece of the drawer slip timber. Set the guide fence on the router so that the groove will line up with the groove on the drawer front.

4 Replace the grooving bit in the router with a rebating bit and set the depth to match the thickness of the drawer side. The top of the rebate should be level with the top of the groove. Make at least two passes with the router, each time increasing the width of the cut until the full width has been achieved.

5 Cut the drawer slip piece the correct length to fit inside the drawer at the front and extend the full length of the drawer side. Use a tenon saw to make a cut out that will allow the the slip to fit over the drawer back.

6 Apply a little adhesive to the face of the rebate and cramp the drawer slip piece in position on the side.

7 When the adhesive has dried, the old drawer bottoms will need to be re-sized to fit into the new drawer slips. The bottom of this drawer was made from solid timber that was only 5 mm thick. Nails had been driven through it, restricting the timber's movement and causing splitting along the length. It needed to be replaced entirely. A new drawer bottom was cut from 6 mm medium density fibreboard (6 mm plywood

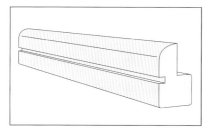

5 Cut the drawer slip piece the correct length to fit inside the drawer at the front and extend along the side.

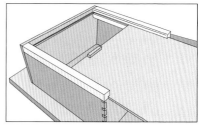

8 Slide the new drawer bottom in place, then fix it down at the back with flat-head nails.

could have been used instead). Cut the new bottom to the new size, allowing for the drawer slips.

8 Slide the drawer bottom back into position and secure it down firmly at the back with flat head nails or with 5/8 in x 4 gauge countersunk screws.

9 Use a smoothing plane to make the slip flush with the sides and the bottom edges.

10 Following the procedure described above, attach a drawer slip to the other side of the drawer.

REPAIRING THE WORN RUNNERS

Along with the drawer sides, the runners were badly worn and needed to be replaced. Before you begin repairs, inspect the runners to see if they have guides fixed to them. Some runners are rebated, so they act as both guide and runner.

1 With a pencil, mark the position of the runners on the cabinet.

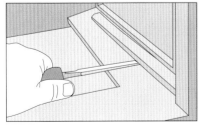

2 Remove each of the drawer runners by inserting the blade of a chisel under it and carefully levering it out.

EQUIPMENT (REPAIRING THE RUNNERS)

- Runner material to match existing sizes
- Material for drawer guides (if necessary)
- Tin of plastic filler
- Sheet of 100-grit abrasive paper
- Candle or a bar of soap
- Slot or cross-head screwdriver
- Tenon saw, jigsaw, panel saw or portable power saw
- Pincers
- Putty knife
- Hammer
- Smoothing plane
- Hammer
- 25 mm chisel
- Wood rasp (if applicable)

2 Inspect the runners to determine how they have been attached to the cabinet. If they have been nailed and glued, slice each joint between the runner and the cabinet at the top and the bottom using a utility knife. Then use a hammer and chisel to lever the runner out. If the runners have been screwed and glued, remove the screws then slice each joint using the same procedure as for nailed and glued joints. If the means of attachment is not obvious, the joints may be tongue and groove. If this is the case, make a diagonal cut across each runner with a tenon saw, then remove the runner. If the runners are glued as well, you may

HINT

Another method of repairing worn runners is to fill the hollows with a plastic filler. To do this, mix a little plastic filler and smooth it into the recess with a putty knife. Plastic filler starts to set in about 5 minutes, so you will need to mix and apply it in batches. When you have filled the recess entirely and the plastic filler has fully hardened, sand the surface flat with 100-grit or coarser abrasive paper or flatten the surface using a wood rasp. Before inserting the drawer, use a straight edge to check that the surface of the runner is flat and square to the face of the unit.

need to break the bond of the adhesive. If the chest of drawers was made in the second half of the twentieth century, the drawer runners may have been stapled onto the drawer and you will need to remove these staples to detach the drawer runners.

3 Using a saw and a smoothing plane, cut and dress the new runner material to the size required. If the originals were only wide enough to support the drawer sides and you have attached drawer slips, you will need to make the runners wide enough to accommodate the slips as well as the sides.

4 Mark the length of the runners then cut to size. If the originals were attached by means of tongue and groove joints cut them long enough to allow this, then cut the tongue joints needed. Runners on drawers in antique pieces should be screwed on and not glued so that they can be adjusted easily or even removed later and replaced when they wear out.

5 Insert the drawer into its opening in the cabinet and then use a smoothing plane to adjust the fit. Apply a little candle wax or a bit of soap to the bottom of each of the drawer runners to make sure that the drawer slides open and closed smoothly.

4 Place the runner on the drawer bottom and with a pencil mark its length, then cut to size.

5 Use a smoothing plane to adjust the fit of the runners to ensure that the drawer slides open and closed easily.

EQUIPMENT (REPAIRING THE BOTTOM)

- Piece of 3 mm plywood
- PVA adhesive
- 30–40 mm panel pins
- Tape measure
- Square
- Tenon saw, panel saw or jigsaw

6 Nail and glue small pieces of plywood or solid timber to the front blade or to the end of each runner to ensure that the drawer closes flush with the face of the chest of drawers.

REPAIRING THE BOTTOM OF THE DRAWER

The bottom of this drawer was too thin, causing it to sag under the weight of the clothes it held. Eventually, the drawer bottom fell out of the frame.

One way to fix this problem is to keep the old bottom and add another layer. This doubles the thickness of the drawer bottom and reduces sagging.

1 Check the joints in the drawer and make sure they are secure.

2 If a joint is loose, knock it apart and apply a little adhesive to it. Then secure the joint using 30–40 mm panel pins while the adhesive sets. Make sure that the drawer bottom is in place before securing the joint.

3 Punch the panel pins below the surface. Check that the drawer is square by measuring each diagonal distance from corner to corner.

4 While the adhesive in the joints is drying, measure the inside dimensions of the drawer with a tape measure.

5 With the tape measure, a square and a pencil, mark the length and width of each side on a piece of 3 mm plywood.

6 Use either a tenon saw, a panel saw or a jigsaw to cut the plywood to size.

7 If you haven't already done so, flex the drawer bottom and pop it back into the grooves.

8 Glue and cramp timber pieces to the underside of the drawer bottom front, back and sides.

9 When the adhesive has set, plane the timber flush with the bottom of the sides of the drawer.

10 Turn the drawer the right way up. Clean up the edges on the new false drawer bottom and drop it in on top of the old one.

11 Put the drawer back in the cabinet and rub a candle or a piece of soap along the drawer runners to ensure that the drawer slides open and closed easily.

Replacing broken hinges

Hinges are commonly used to join moveable sections of a piece of furniture. Replacing broken hinges requires no expertise and only a little time.

EQUIPMENT

- Hinges
- Slot-head or cross-head screwdriver
- Hammer
- 25 mm chisel
- 12 mm chisel
- Smoothing plane
- Cabinet scraper
- Sanding cork
- Bradawl
- Marking gauge
- Utility knife

REMOVING THE OLD HINGES

1 Decide what type of hinges are needed—the pair on this table were made of steel. Brass hinges will not rust like steel hinges. Stainless steel is a good option but these hinges are hard to obtain—some specialty hardware suppliers and ship's chandlers stock them. Choose a longer pair of hinges with a narrow leaf if you cannot match the size

2 Remove the old hinges. If the screws are very rusty, this may be difficult, as the heads may break off and the slots disintegrate. It's a good idea to apply a little lubricant spray and wait a while before attempting extraction. If a screw is still tight, tapping the screwdriver with a hammer will help to loosen its grip.

3 Place the new material in a vice. Align a leaf of the hinge with the outside of the existing recess and mark its length on the other end with a utility knife or a chisel. Set a marking gauge the width of a leaf to the centre of the knuckle and gauge the width of the leaf on the table's edge. Repeat the process for all the replacement hinges and their recesses.

REPLACING THE HINGES

4 With a hammer and chisel, cut down to the thickness of one leaf and clean out the waste from the open side of the recess. Make sure that the flat back of the chisel is facing

3 Align the leaf of a hinge with the outside of the existing recess and mark its length with a chisel.

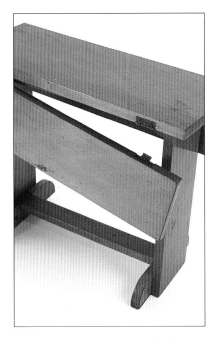

One hinge of this table had come loose and all had rust damage.

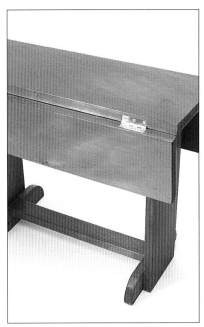

Brass hinges, which will not rust, were chosen as replacements.

towards the outside of the recess. The depth of the recess should be similar to the original. If you need to cut the recess deeper to ensure that the leaf is flush with the surface, keep a close check on the depth. If you cut the recess too deep, the hinge's

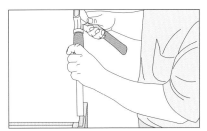

4 Using a hammer and chisel, cut down to the thickness of one leaf of the hinge.

movement will be restricted and the two table leaves will bind and not open flat. This will weaken the screws holding the hinge and the hinges will come loose. If the recesses are cut too deep, use packing to keep the hinge leaves flush with the surface.

5 Form a pilot holes for the screws, using a bradawl or a drill bit slightly smaller than the screws' shanks. Drill the pilot holes off-centre so that when the screws are countersunk the hinge is pulled tightly to the back of the recess. Make sure that the screw heads fit flush with the surface of the hinge leaf.

Replacing a cane seat

Cane chair seats come in two types: those that are woven—a job for a professional—and those that are laid as a sheet. Replacing a sheet cane seat looks difficult but is really quite simple to do.

EQUIPMENT

- Piece of cane sheeting 450 x 450 mm
- Length of 4 mm pith cane
- PVA adhesive
- Putty
- Sheet of 180-grit abrasive paper
- Sheet of 240-grit abrasive paper
- 500 ml clear acrylic lacquer
- Hammer
- 14 mm chisel with a maximum thickness of 6 mm
- Utility knife
- Spokeshave or wood rasp
- Pencil brush
- Router with 6 mm straight cutter and template guide (optional)
- Two quick action cramps (optional)
- Two sash cramps (optional)

CONVERTING FROM WOVEN TO SHEET CANE

Weaving a cane seat is a job for experts. It is possible, however, to convert a seat from the type supporting woven cane to one with sheet cane. To do this, make a template the required shape. Cramp the template to the seat frame, and then use a router with a template cutter to cut a groove 6 mm wide and 6 mm deep around the frame.

TYPES OF CANE SEAT

1 Before you can replace the seat, you need to establish if the cane is woven or is laid as a sheet. A seat that has cane laid as a sheet will have a groove around the frame, usually with strands of broken cane protruding from it. A woven cane seat, however, will have a row of holes around the perimeter of the seat frame.

REPLACING SHEET CANE

2 Before replacing the cane sheeting, you must ensure that the frame of the seat is strong enough to support it. Check the joints to determine whether they are intact. If they are loose, take the frame apart and reglue the joints using the appropriate adhesive. Strip old finish from the piece, sand each part and assemble.

3 With a utility knife, cut away any remaining cane strands from the groove. Then use a 4 mm chisel to remove the pith cane from the groove. Hold the chisel with the bevelled face down and take care when removing pith from the corners of the groove.

The cane insert in the centre of the chair's seat had disintegrated and needed replacing with new cane sheet.

The new sheet cane insert made the chair functional again. The area around the insert was retouched.

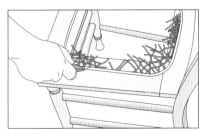

3 With a utility knife, cut away any remaining cane strands from the groove around the seat.

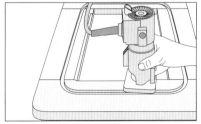

5 Use a router with a roundover bit, a spokeshave or a wood rasp to form a round on the groove's inside edges.

PREPARING THE CANE SHEET

4 Soak both the new cane sheet and the pith cane in a tub of water for at least an hour so that it becomes soft and pliable and it expands.

5 Check the inside edges of the seat frame to make sure that they are well rounded and have a radius of 6 mm or greater. If they don't, use a spokeshave, a wood rasp or a router with a 10 mm roundover bit and attached bearing to form a round.

LAYING THE CANE SHEET

6 Shape a piece of 6 x 20 mm long timber so that one edge is bowed and the corners are rounded over.

7 Place adhesive in the groove in the seat frame using a glue bottle and spread the adhesive in the groove. Lay the cane sheeting square over the seat frame, with a 50 mm overhang all around.

8 Starting at the centre of the groove at the back, lay the pith on top of the

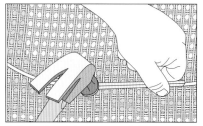

8 Lay the pith on top of the cane and tap it and the cane into the groove using a hammer and the timber piece.

cane and tap it and the cane into the groove using a hammer and the timber piece. Use the rounded over ends of the timber to work your way around the corner. Then rub the stick firmly along the pith cane to smooth it out and push it just below the level of the frame.

9 When you have worked the pith cane into the groove around the entire perimeter of the seat, cut the pith cane and push the end of it into the groove.

10 Remove any excess adhesive with a wet rag and leave the cane to dry overnight.

FINISHING

11 Overnight the cane should dry and shrink and next morning the surface should be tight and drummy. Trim the excess on the outside of the pith with the utility knife.

12 Place putty in any holes, dents or bruises on the frame around the seat and give the seat frame a final sand. Apply at least two coats of a surface finish to the seat frame.

13 The chair featured for this project was finished with clear acrylic lacquer; you may prefer painting the chair and leaving the cane unpainted. If you do, paint the frame before applying the cane. A clear, protective coating should be applied to the cane to ward off dirt and make the cane easier to clean.

FITTING PADDED SEATS AND REPLACING RAILS

PADDED SEATS

Many upright chairs have padded instead of cane seats. To replace this type of seat, follow these steps.

1 Remove the damaged seat with pincers, a hammer and a chisel. Pull out any nails or punch them below the surface.

2 Make a paper template of the shape of the seat and check its fit. Transfer the template to 10–12 mm plywood and cut out the shape. Cut the shape in foam and glue it to the plywood. Cover the foam with thick calico, pulling it tight and stapling it to the bottom of the plywood. Cover with fabric.

RAILS

The rails of upright chairs often snap off and need replacing. To fit a new rail between chair legs, follow these steps.

1 Check that all the legs are secure. If any are loose, detach and label each leg so that they can be replaced in the correct position. Scrape the old adhesive off each leg then apply new adhesive to the socket and the end of the leg. Press the leg firmly into the socket and cramp the chair together until the adhesive has dried.

2 Measure the distance between the leg, plus the depth of one hole (which the rail will fit into). Cut a piece of dowelling rod this length. Put a little adhesive into each hole, fit one end of the rail into one hole, then work the other end into the other hole. Centre the rail and leave the adhesive to dry.

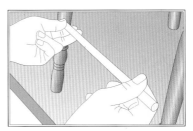

2 To fit a new rail, place the rail into one hole, then in the other hole, and centre it.

The frame and legs as well as the body of the chair contained sections where the seagrass had come loose.

The new seagrass is slightly darker than the existing but will fade to match with time.

Repairing unravelled seagrass

Seagrass chairs come in a number of styles, so repairs must be considered on the basis of the chair. However, provided the cane frames and wicker spokes are sound, it is easy to repair these chairs.

PREPARATION

1 Study the construction of the chair and the weaving pattern. Leave at least one leg of the chair wrapped to provide a guide for wrapping the other legs. Cut a small sample of loose seagrass from your chair and take it to a cane supplier to match its

EQUIPMENT

- One or more skeins of seagrass
- Panel tacks with large heads or staples for a staple gun
- PVA adhesive
- Staple gun (optional)
- Scissors
- Hammer

size. Seagrass comes in different widths and can be purchased from cane suppliers. Addresses for these can be found in your telephone directory (possibly under cane or bamboo). Note that the seagrass for the seat and the binding of the legs may be different widths. The new seagrass will be a different colour from the weathered strands but will change over time to become similar.

WEAVING THE NEW STRANDS OF SEAGRASS

2 To replace a section, cut the seagrass where you want to insert the new strands. Working towards the front of the seat, unpick the short lengths of the old strands. Take the

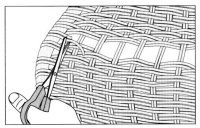

2 To replace a section, first cut the old seagrass where you want to insert new strands.

remaining cut end to the back of the seat after it passes over the spoke, leaving a tail of about 50 mm.

3 Each row of the seagrass seat is woven using two strands of seagrass. At the beginning of one row, the seagrass is woven over the first spoke and under the second, then at the beginning of the next row, it is woven under the first spoke and over the next.

4 Take a piece of new seagrass (the length will depend on the amount of weaving you want to replace) and fold it in half to form a loop consisting of two strands. Insert the loop through the seat after the next spoke. Slip the loop over the cut ends of the worn section of seagrass and weave under and over the spokes to the frame, keeping a firm tension on the seagrass.

5 Wrap the seagrass around the frame twice—to the right of the strand—and then come up under frame on the left and commence the next row.

6 Continue removing the damaged seagrass a little at a time and weaving in the new strands until you come to a section that is not worn.

JOINING AND ENDING STRANDS

7 To join in new strands, form a loop with the new strands and secure the cut ends of the previous strands

by slipping the loop of the new strands over them.

8 To finish the strands, poke them through to the wrong side, leaving a 25 mm tail. The seagrass will tighten naturally and hold the strands in place. Alternatively, you could finish at the side frame binding by sliding the cut ends under the existing binding and fixing with a tack.

9 Turn the chair over and trim any long seagrass tails secured by loops to about 15 mm.

BINDING THE LEGS

10 To bind the legs, bend about 100 mm of seagrass at a right angle to the strand. Smear the leg with a little PVA adhesive.

11 Starting at the top of the leg, place the bent section against the leg and bind the seagrass over it. Keeping each line of wrapped seagrass firmly pushed against the previous one, wrap the lines of seagrass down to about 50 mm from the end of the leg.

FINISHING THE LEGS

12 On the last round, take the seagrass under the previous round and pull upwards. Do this on the inside of the chair leg where it will not show.

13 Secure the seagrass by applying a little PVA adhesive and inserting a panel tack.

CARING FOR SEAGRASS

To keep a piece of seagrass furniture looking good, follow these maintenance tips.

• Seagrass likes humid conditions but is not designed for the outdoors. Water should be dried from it immediately.

• It should be dusted regularly with a soft cloth or brush or vaccuumed using the brush attachment to the vaccuum-cleaner. Nooks and crevices can be brushed with a soft-bristled toothbrush.

• Every few months, wipe a seagrass piece with a soft damp cloth and apply a little furniture polish to maintain and protect it.

• To clean a dirty seagrass chair, mix a little detergent with water and apply with a sponge. Rinse with fresh water by spraying with a hose or placing under a shower. Then dry quickly by putting the piece outside in a windy or sunny spot or by fanning it with a hair dryer or convection heater. Allow a few days to elapse before sitting on the chair to prevent damage to the chair's seat.

• 'Natural' seagrass is, as the term implies, a natural product, but the seagrass is often artificially stained or coated with a light coat of varnish, shellac or lacquer. To retouch natural seagrass, clean it and then apply a coat of the appropriate finish.

Tools for repairing furniture

Some of the most useful tools for repairing furniture are shown below. Build up your tool kit gradually—most of the tools can be purchased from your local hardware store.

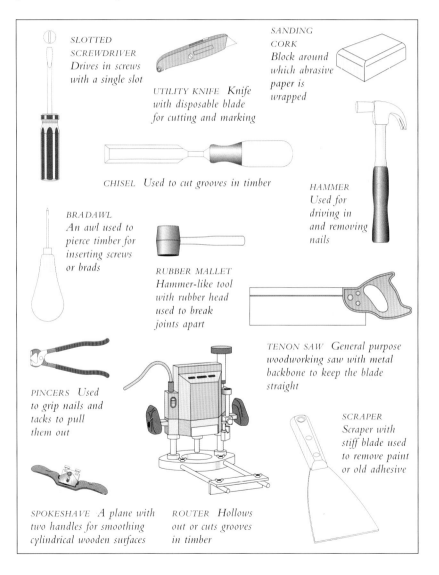

SLOTTED SCREWDRIVER *Drives in screws with a single slot*

UTILITY KNIFE *Knife with disposable blade for cutting and marking*

SANDING CORK *Block around which abrasive paper is wrapped*

CHISEL *Used to cut grooves in timber*

HAMMER *Used for driving in and removing nails*

BRADAWL *An awl used to pierce timber for inserting screws or brads*

RUBBER MALLET *Hammer-like tool with rubber head used to break joints apart*

TENON SAW *General purpose woodworking saw with metal backbone to keep the blade straight*

PINCERS *Used to grip nails and tacks to pull them out*

SCRAPER *Scraper with stiff blade used to remove paint or old adhesive*

SPOKESHAVE *A plane with two handles for smoothing cylindrical wooden surfaces*

ROUTER *Hollows out or cuts grooves in timber*

Index